# Going on vacation

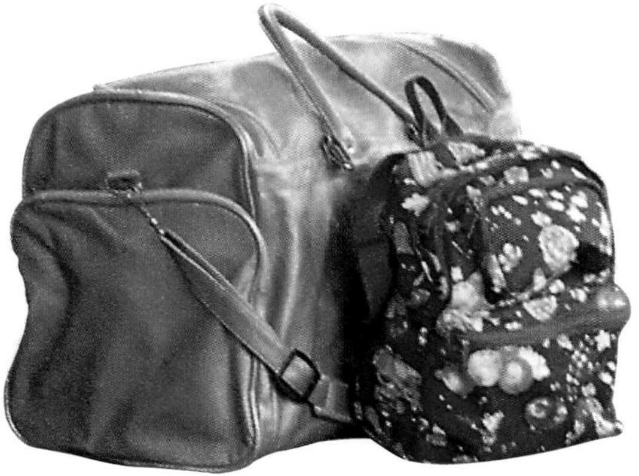

We go on a train.

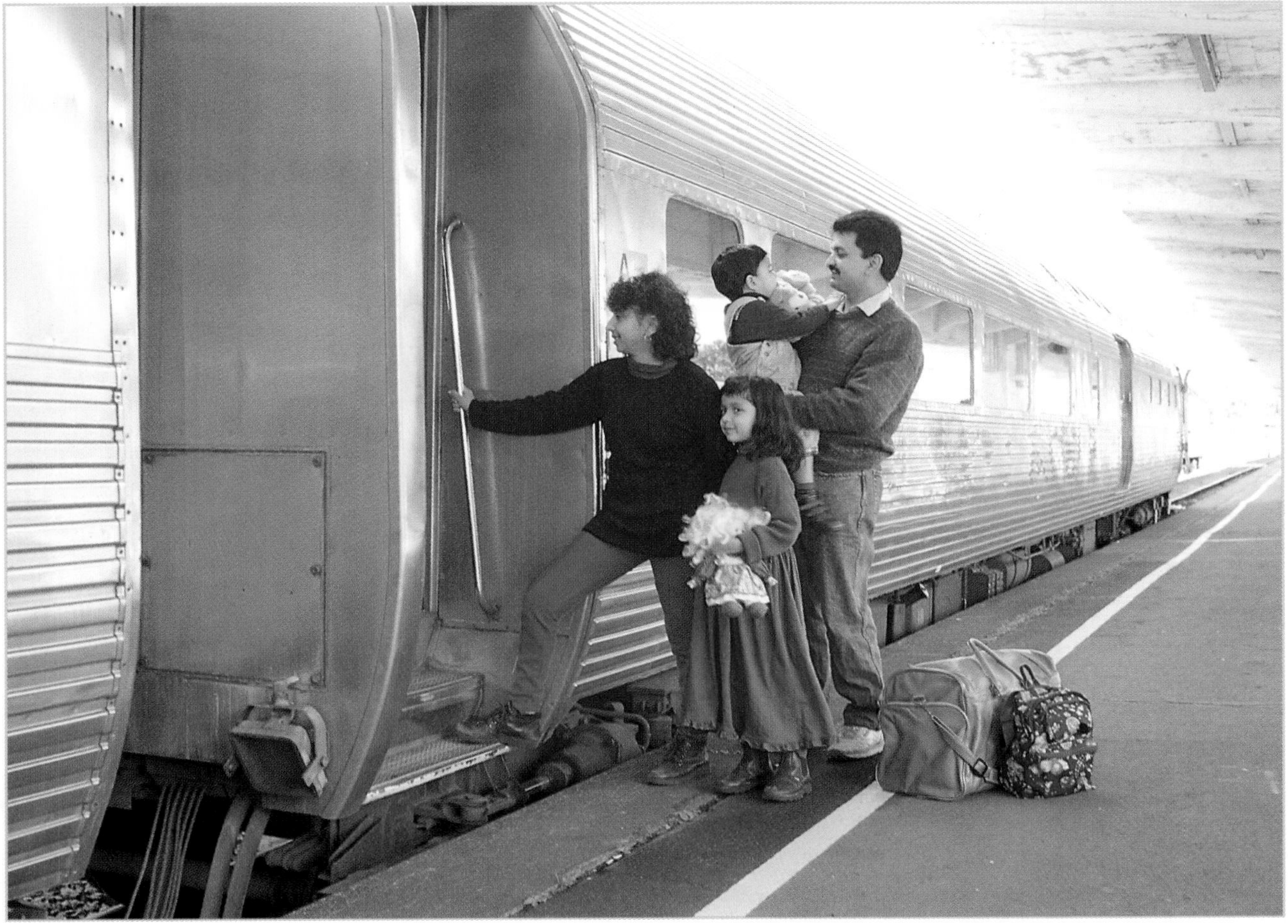

We go on a bus.

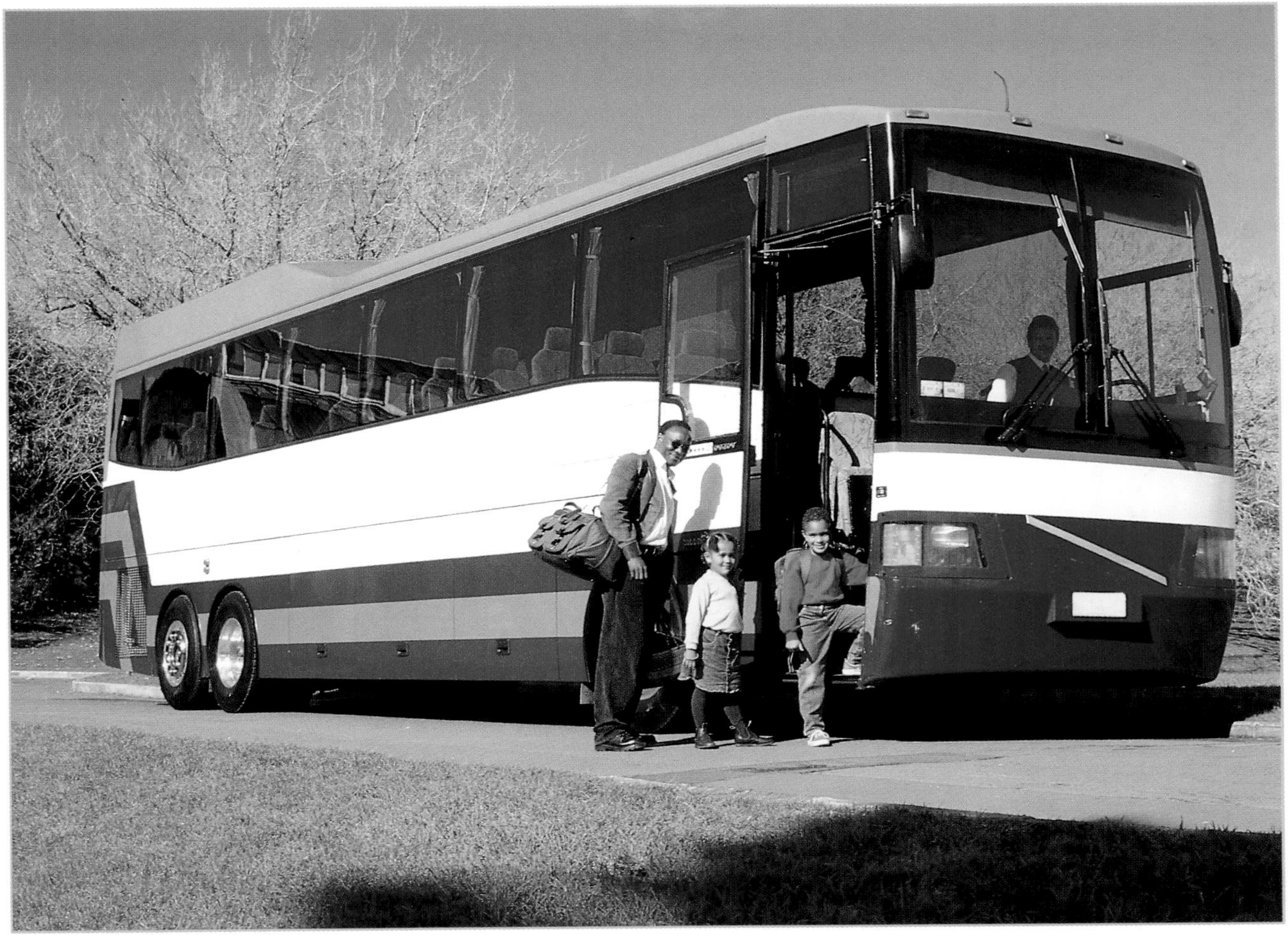

We go in a car.

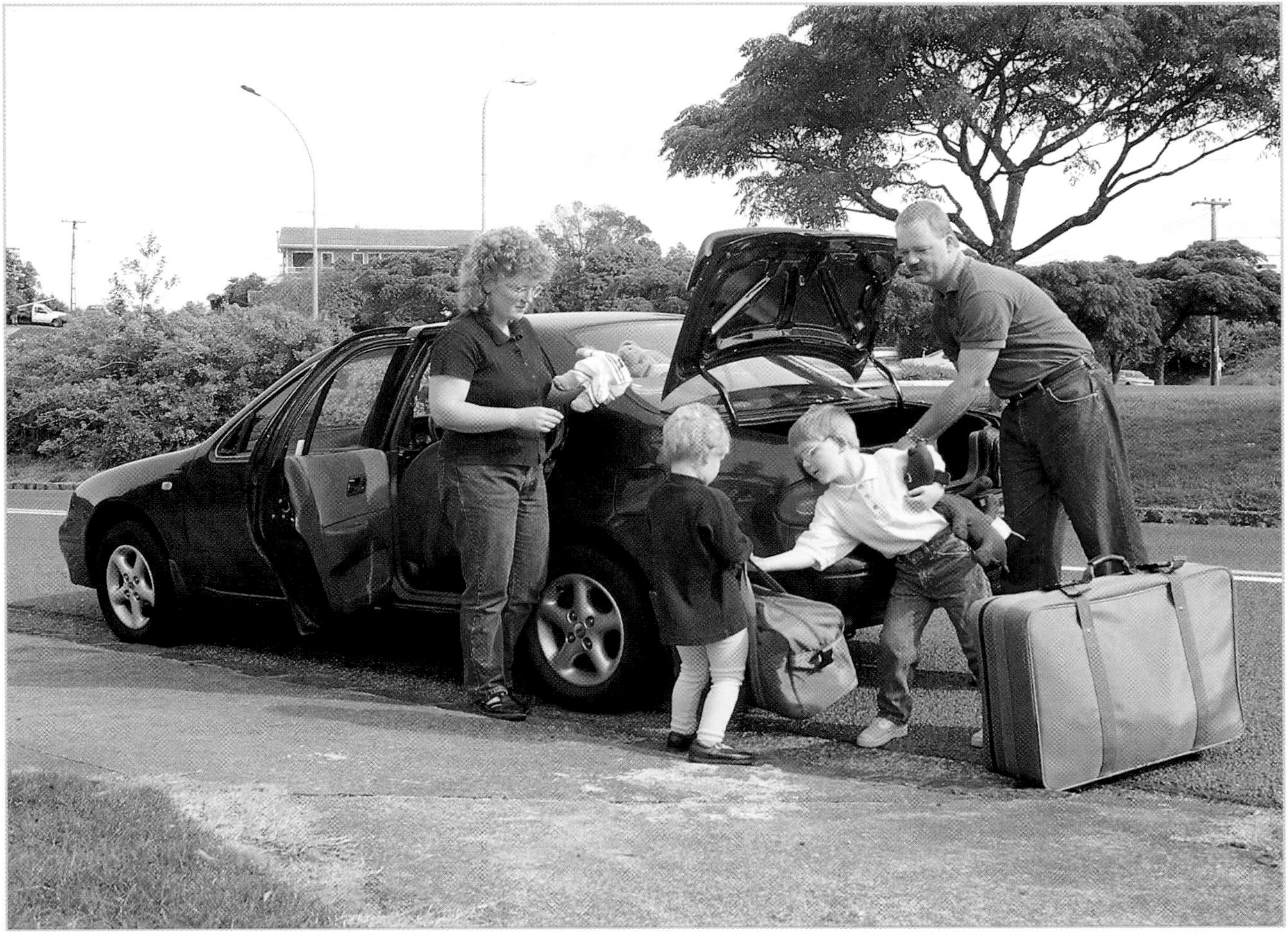

We go in a van.

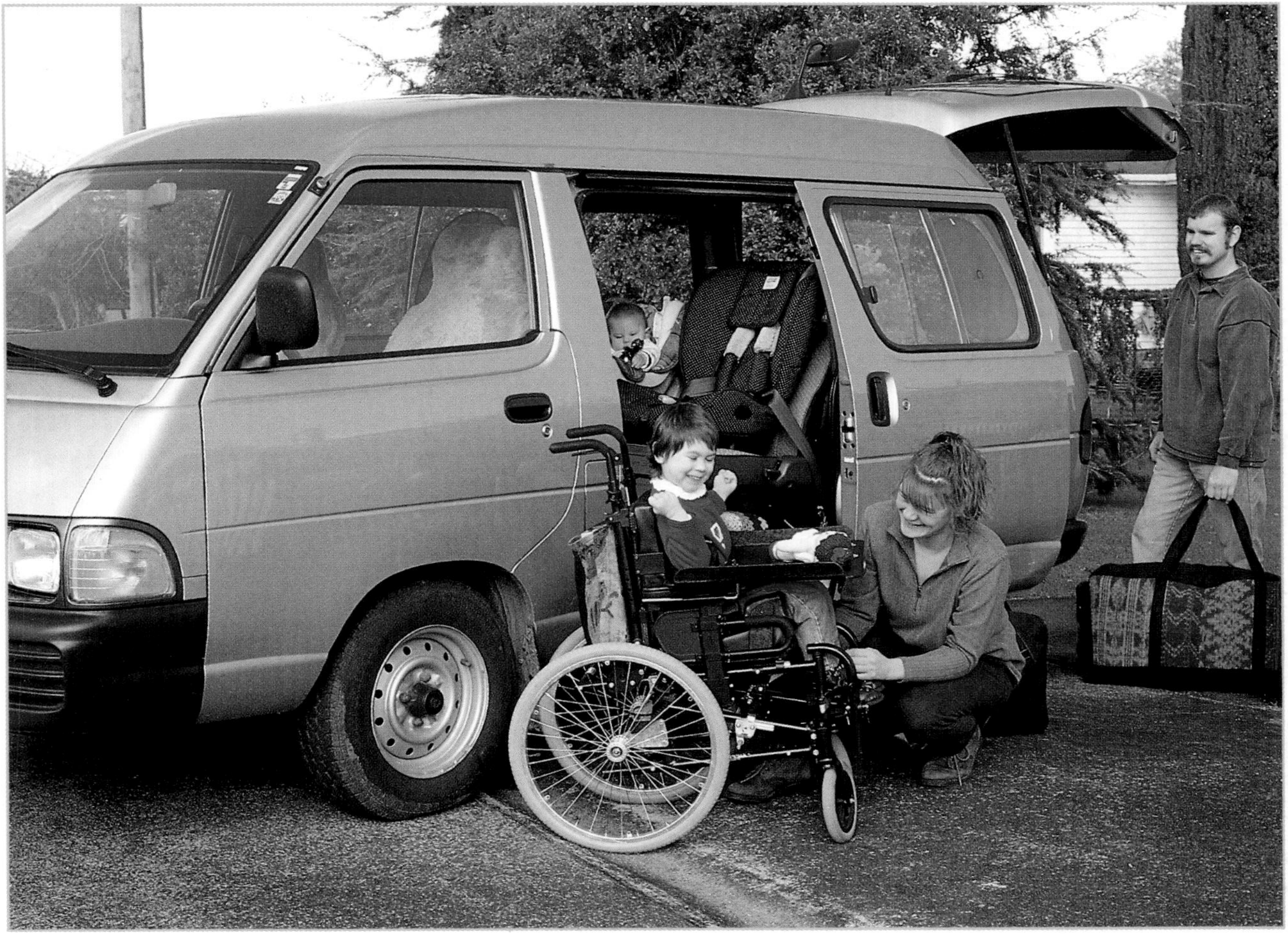

We go on a boat.

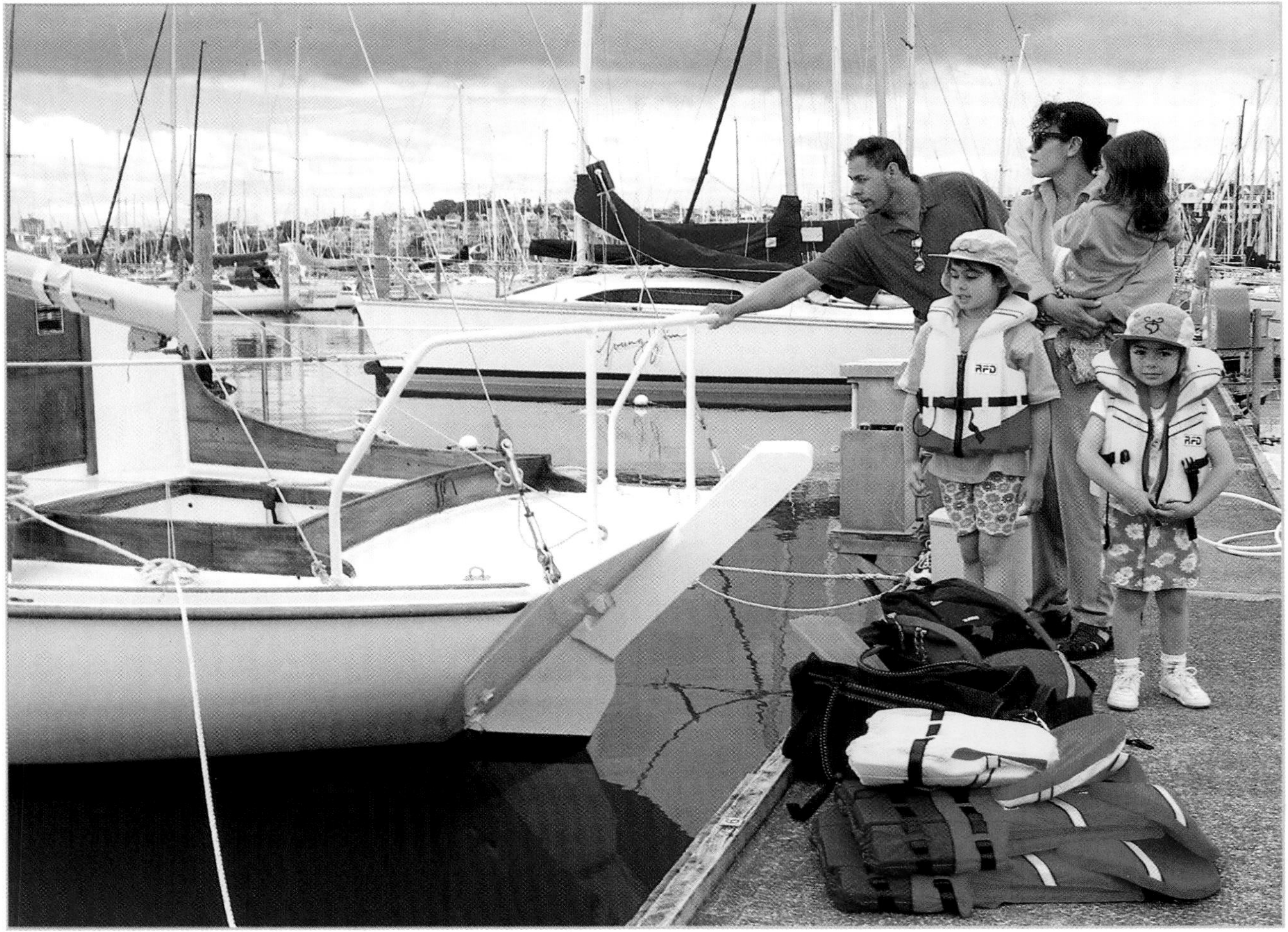
RFD
RFD

We go in a truck.

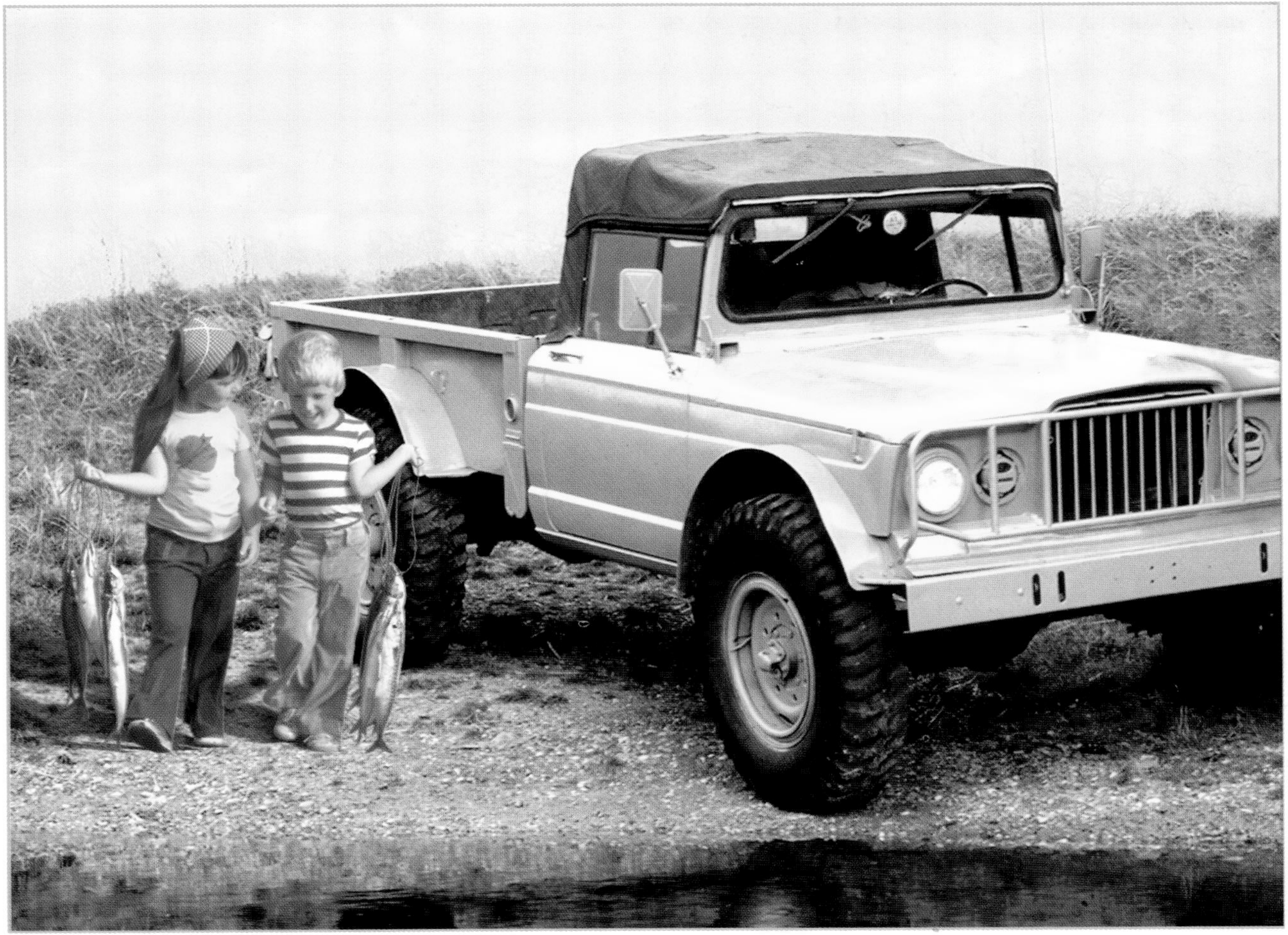

We go in a camper.

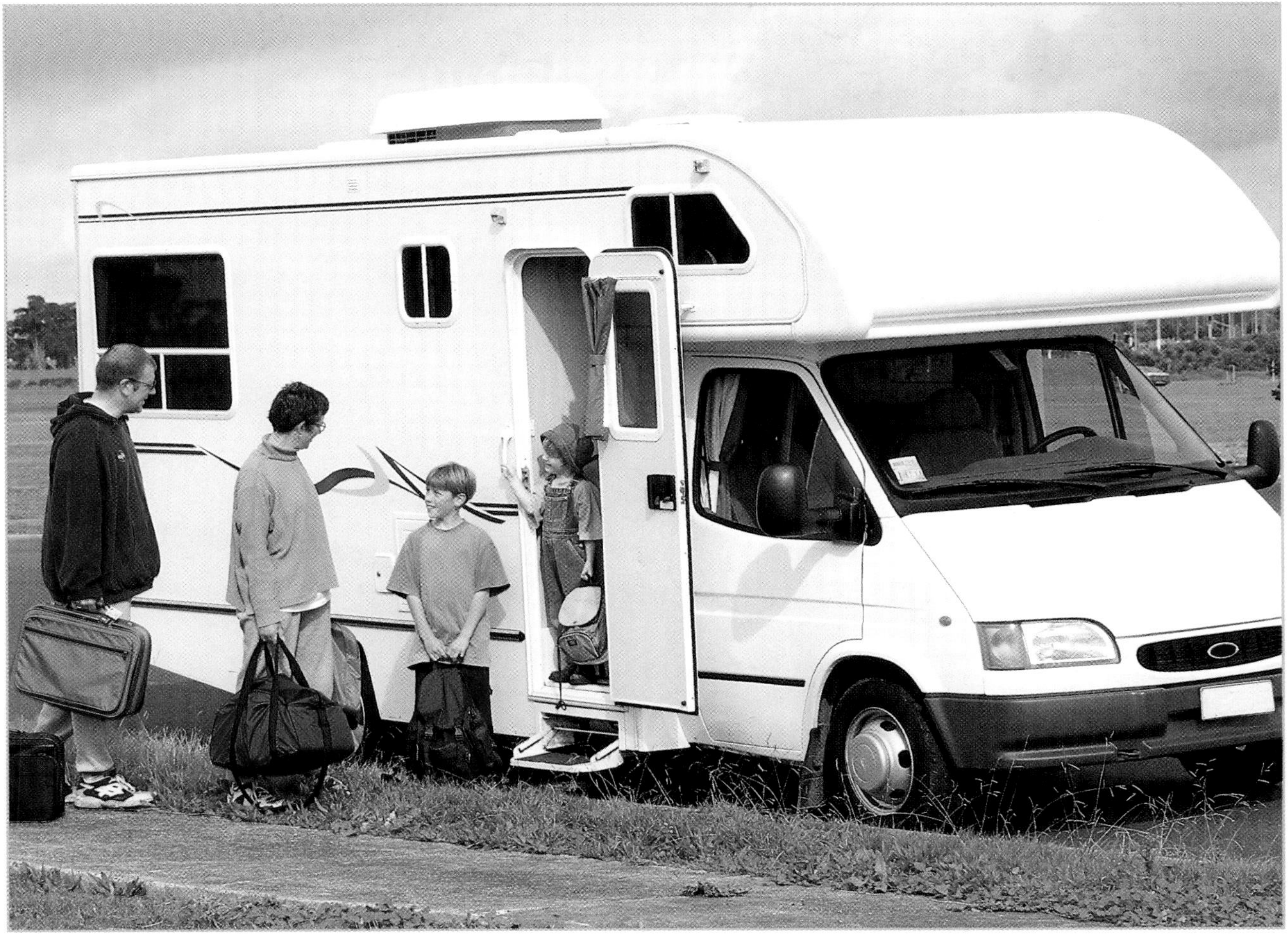

We go on a plane.

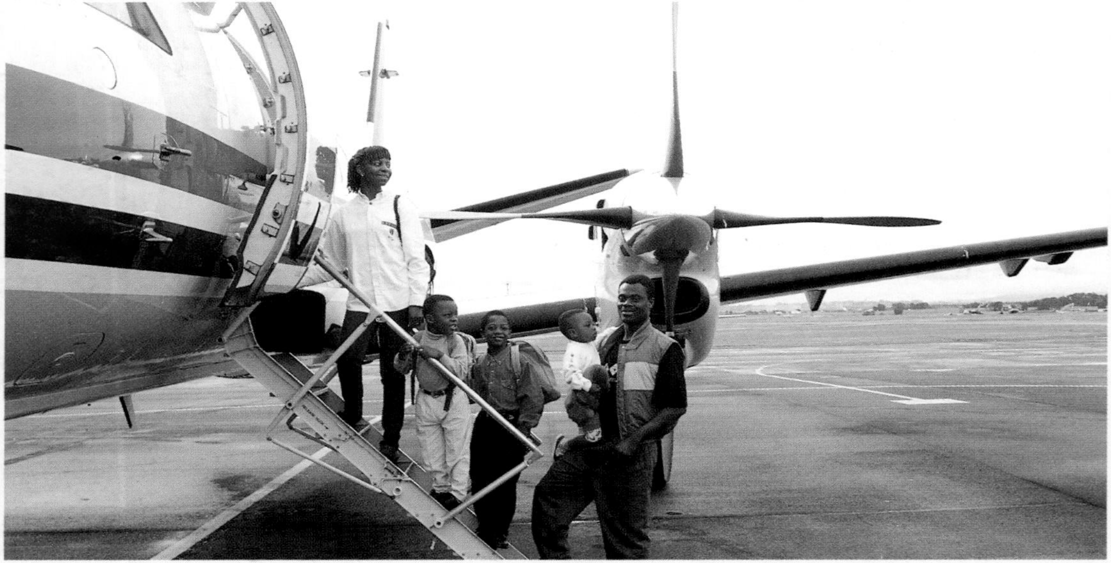